ERMINA AFROZ

ENCOMIUM

ISBN: 9798391631897
Cover design by Parvathi Raj A
source: @parvathiiraj

Illustrations by Zainab Shabir
source: @benaam_zs

Printed in India by Kindle Direct Publishing
First printing edition 2023

For Abbu,
in the loving memory
of his undying spirit

ENCOMIUM

If it didn’t hurt,
it is always so beautiful
to return back
to a person,
a place,
a memory.

Thank you
for returning back to me.

-from the author of comma.

ABBU
ABBU

ENCOMIUM

I could write in apparent details.
The sky rained tears.
I entered home and ran to your room
but my trembling hand couldn't unlock it.
The smell of jannat-ul-firdaus
filled every corner of the now haunting house.
If I shut close my eyes,
I feel the long drawn out bite of your frozen hands.
The plastics had carved a deeper scar down the cheeks.
And some untreated wound still oozed out blood from your side.
You were blue.
I ran up to grab your best ironed clothes,
but you preferred a crumbled white shroud.
There was noise,
but you weren't listening to anything.
Not even I called for you, "....abbu? Abbu? Abbu?..."
and then there was your body
but I couldn't see your face
and then seconds later I was standing in an empty room.
And in that emptiness
I told you,
Allah Hafiz,
I love you.

ENCOMIUM

I want sadness, happiness
fury, order
mess, immaculateness
madness, lucidity
I want to be the magnet,
with the opposite natures of my poles.
I want to be repulsive,
attractive,
the full bar.

I grudge the moon to see you wail.
Atleast someone permits you to be vulnerable.

-Men

Memories fade away
because unlike certitude
which is devised on facts and actual truths,
memories are devised of illusions,
imageries,
fantasies,
longings,
a past,
and the past needs to leave,
it needs to bid adieu.
Let it do so.

It can all get messy,
always
And yet you so see how mighty hope is,
Even the few grains of sand left in my palm
Can still make me smile.
That a little something,
someday,
will stay.

ENCOMIUM

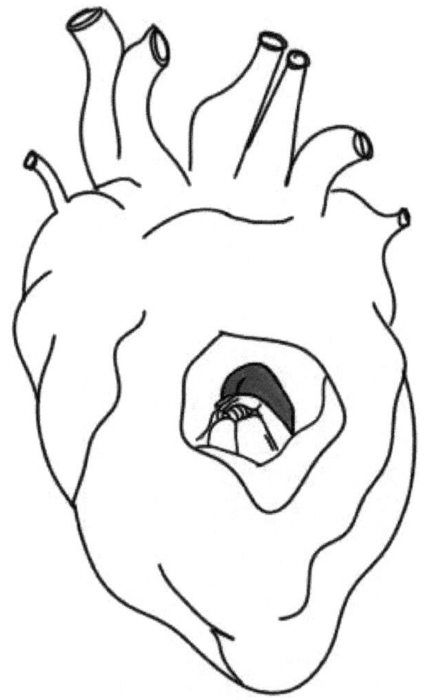

The curiosity I have to learn more about you
doesn't match the feeling of having known you
completely since I ever saw you.
Which is to say,
I know exactly the way you smile with a shyness that
glitters in your eyes,
but I need to learn the sound of your laughter.
I know exactly the color of your dreamy
compassionate yet scared eyes,
but I need to learn about the places you search for to
hide them when you cannot directly look at me.
I know exactly how warm your generous palms feel
against my skin,
but I need to learn how to help you to unclench them
and not be weighed down by trying to hold every
sorrow,
every responsibility,
everything that needs to be gone.
I know exactly the way and pace your heart beats
but I need to learn how to live in it forever and not
break it. And all of this is to say that I know exactly
what you are,
but I need to learn how to make you mine.

ENCOMIUM

If you are ever to love me,
love me like a moon orchid,
keep me from igniting by providing me only the little
warmth I'll need from your ray of sunshine,
don't overflow me with the waters of your
overwhelming care but keep me from dying by giving
the timely heed.
Feed me the right quantity of fertilizer
from the formula of your protection,
but don't limit me within peripheries.
Let me bloom in my space.
If you are ever to love me,
let me bloom like the moon orchid.

ENCOMIUM

One blink of the eye
and I knew you were a snap.

-left, too early

That someone meant for me
will be standing under the street light
with a dead flower in one hand
while the wind blows over their face
and a fluttering book in another
and when they'll look at me they'll know it's right
and that we are children of the Lord,
and we'll exchange greetings in poetries,
and share glances in metaphors
and speak in melodies
and the world will fall silent for a second,
everything will be dark,
it'll only be the starting of an ending
and I'll know whose grave will mine be dug beside
and I'll finally love.

–find me

ENCOMIUM

I write the disappointment of separateness
and eagerness of a meet,
the world fall silent in both the seasons
and there is always a question,
how long?

I see blurry and vague dreams at night
and then I see you and I force its remembrance
and I wake up and I note it down.
I do not,
even accidentally,
want to let it go.
How for a brief moment it felt so real.
I miss it being real.
And so, I want to dream of you every night.

-dreams where Abbu visits me

ENCOMIUM

I am the captor
the prisoner
the prison

keeping myself confined
within the perimeter
I have encircled around me

the society
and you

are not given that advantage from my side
you are but the subservient complexity of my life

I haven't allowed myself to touch the roses
because I'm fearful of the thorns

I haven't allowed myself to burn the candle
because I'm fearful of the light

and how ironical, you see
both pain and beauty
only know how to hurt me

my home I've made a prison
my room, people visit but I do not move out

ENCOMIUM

are crimes contagious?
If yes, stay away
for I've committed a crime
better communicated as sin

I am the captor
the prisoner
the prison

your living
equalizes my survival
for we both breath
just you the air of freedom,
me the pollution of crisis

I am the captor
the prisoner
the prison

and unlike any other
I do not ask for bail
neither for total freedom
I'm just fine within these walls
the world out there isn't for me.

The choices that you make for yourself
May not always be in the favor
of everyone else as well.
Nevertheless,
it doesn't make it any less better for you.

They say sorry is a powerful word.
Yet I find mine searching its worth.
How small a fault does sorry make right?
Does not returning love count?

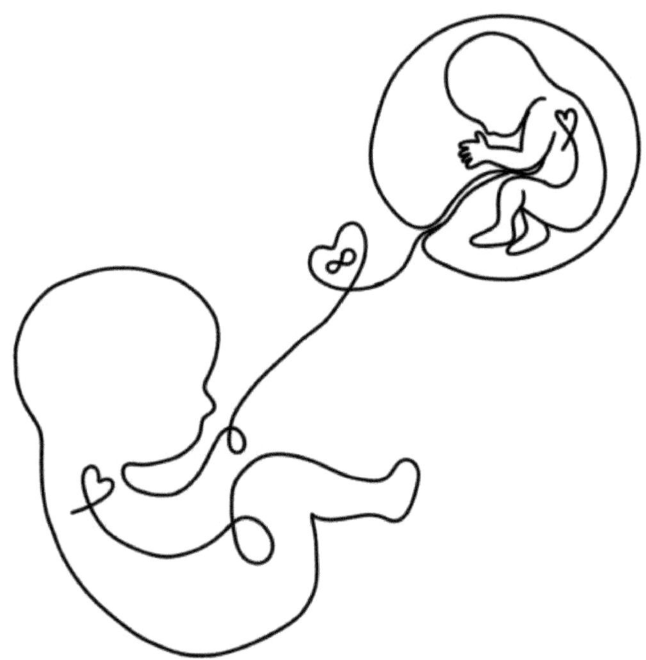

I love how words rhyme.
And how there are certain people in this world
who have their doppelgangers.
I love how two people can be born together
and have identical faces.
And how someone can inherit someone's look
by sharing genes.
And yet to realize the mournful reality
of not having anyone to resonate with.

-alone|lonely

I think I'm a lunatic.
I think of things that haven't happened
or those that do not personally have a possibility of
occurring. Because I smell flowers and remember
their essence
like it's of a long lost love.
Because most days I question myself,
"who am I"
and love myself for being uncertain.
Because I drop hot wax down my fingers
and consider its warmth close to the feel of the sun.
Because I hear my chest pounding
and sing lyrics to the tune of it.
Because I twirl around stacks of unfinished canvases
and imagine them to be painted by the flow of my
moves. Because I feel pain so deep
that I do not sometimes feel at all.
Because I like to let go and then pull it all back
together before it gets out of sight.
I think I'm a lunatic.
Or could I be a poet?
Or is it just the same?

In years of growing up,
I have learnt one but most important virtue of life.
And it spells out as Sabr.
To have patience for a being,
to have patience for the wound to heal,
to have patience for the prayers to be heard
and to have patience while you intent for them.
For Sabr is another weaving of a loom
and cranking through the sewing
only takes away the beauty of it.

-stiches of hope

I stare at my reflection and get horror-stricken.
It makes me palpitate to reflect
that my suppressed side will come to life
and look back at me with cold eyes.
I have killed it within me
and do not intent to kindle its rebirth,
it has but no space in this world
that condemns speech and commands oppression
and I,
for what it is worth,
have learnt survival on the conditions.

- silenced

I heard of a fallacy,
the other person has it worse,
and so I protest,
your feelings are genuine,
are worthy,
and the world is to listen to it when you speak,
being alive,
just as they would to a funeral prayer
for someone who presumably
“had it worse”.

-speak before you are spoken of

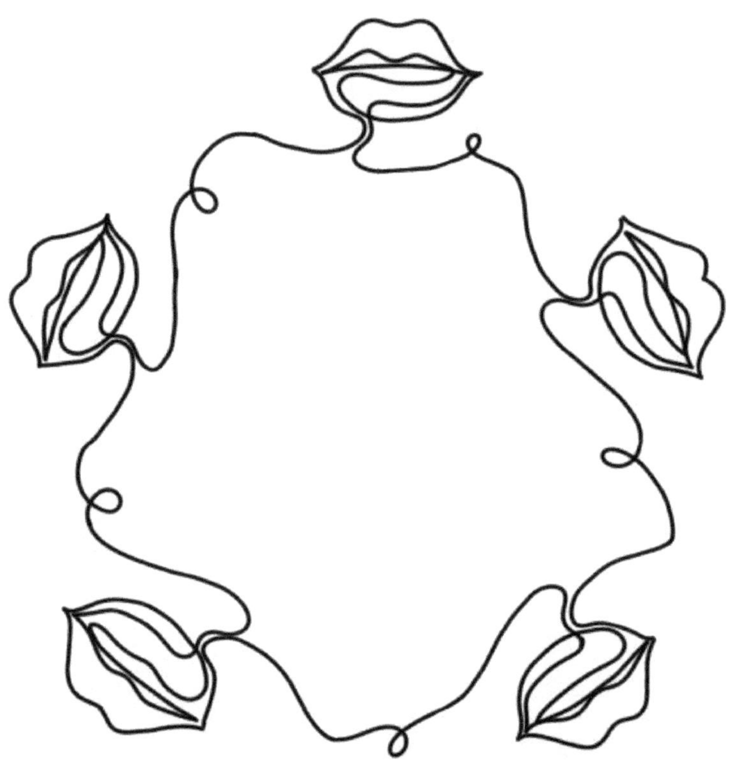

When I look up in the sky,
I see no face,
only an outlying feeling.
So instead I close my eyes and imagine.
The way your laugh would break into little fragments
as if giving each one of us a part of it.
The way your walk was so light footed
so none of us would shockingly wake up.
The way your presence would leave
a long lasting scent of warmth.
But then I open my eyes and everything's dissipated
into a wind that never flew.
Perhaps I should close my eyes forever,
and meet you again.

-see you in heaven

ENCOMIUM

You do not cower before a man, girl.

You've heaven beneath your feet
and mystical potentiality in your tender beautiful palms

You are half of a man's religion
and have eloquence in your speech

You are means for paradise
and you have a whole pallet of hue in your liquid eyes
a cast shaped out of twinkles and glint

So the next time you question your significance,
remember all of them are not even half of you.

What I desired for,
what I prayed for,
what I sobbed for,
what I lost,
what I bewailed,
what I have now- it's this that I am.
It's this that defines me.
So to ask of who I am is what I've been through.

-who are you?

Grief sounds like the noise made by the elevation of the hospital bed into its fowler's position so that my father can sit up and be fed for 90 consecutive days.

Grief sounds like the heavy sighs my mother takes inclusive of calling out loud to God for his mercy upon His children and his better half at odds of the night.

Grief sounds like the suppressed sighs and wails I make at the funeral of my close ones.

Grief sounds like the call an old lady makes at my doorstep everyday begging for money and food to continue her daily survival.

Grief sounds like the rolling tires of a vendor's handcart when he beckons people to purchase his products while the roads are empty and people sit within their homes.

Grief sounds like the sob of a wife who lost her husband while he fought a battle that no one knew the end of.

ENCOMIUM

Grief sounds like a mother who cried to see his child one last time before her own soul departed to the Heavens.

Grief sounds heavy,
grief sounds throbbing,
grief sounds of loss
grief sounds shocking.
Grief- is mutually felt.
And yet, so personal?!

-my grief stories of 2021.

The most human trait I incorporate
is that of creating art and being an artist,
and living nature and loving nature,
of reading books and writing poetries,
of witnessing emotions and expressing emotions.
For riches,
substances,
and customs
are merely possessions for the bone,
and love
gratitude
acknowledgement
that of the soul.

You feel enormously elated to be the listening ear,
but your own prayers, you hold back.
You feel obliged to be instinctively aware,
yet your own sensibilities, you hold back.
You berth everyone on devoted revere,
yet your designations, you hold back.
Tell me why do you give the world everything,
but yourself, you hold back?

There is no address I have in this new city that I now reside in,

And I keep running ahead in search of the streets that shall smell of endearment,

Of mom,
of dad's security,

But I find only burnt charcoal,
And smirking men

The shadows of the trees here no more provide shade,
it's a horror I encounter when it sways across my unopened window at night,

I feel alone,
I cry,
I want home,
And it's far.
Far away.

-no place to be

You are not just your name

You are the tea that you pour in shikora cups and
serve your grand mom with her favorite fried meat
pockets,
you are that consideration.

You are the tears you cry in sujood while sending
blessings upon your granddad,
you are that recollection.

You are the mask you protect your father with which
provides him the needed oxygen,
you are that breath.

You are the knife that you cut fruits with for your
mother for the first time when she can't get up from
the bed,
you are that support.

You are those calming words that you speak to your
elder sister when she loses hope and feels smaller
than you,
you are that encouragement.

You are that call that your brother makes to enquire
if everything is fine at home,
you are that responsibility.

You are that gentle hand you wipe over your nieces'
face when she cries after seeing her mother in pain,
you are that care.

You are that belief in your friends' heart when she
reminds you to stay strong,
you are that power.

You are that wish of someone's prayer
You are that hope of someone's living
You are that cane of a fractured heart

You are so much more than your name
You are a whole emotion
You are the whole world.

ABBU

Everybody stood around you,
very dutifully,
the way we would when you accidentally called all of our names while only intending to call one of us.
Today we're all here too but you wouldn't speak.
I pass you a little letter,
the way I did when I was 5,
only this time you didn't read it to laugh at my silly writing.
I didn't know death meant silence too.
For what is chaos? Only your being.
And what was noise but of your laughter.
And now that you wouldn't agree to open your eyes,
I realized death took away you
and also the meaning of existence.

You listen to all my stories
dig inside me
and make me vulnerable
you tell me it's okay to bleed the hurt out
and then you leave me exposed
And Alone.
I'm bandaging
again.

-bandages

Every time I tie my hair up tight
A few strands break and fall down
I'm sorry I shouldn't have held us together so taut.

-strained

Every last of my incarnations inhabit me
and I'm twenty but also two
and I feel I'll need my dad even when I'm 50
while I know he's not here
but it won't stop me from feeling that way
and I'll lure over a candy when I'm 30
because it'll make me remind of sweet hours
and I'll feel the burden of my child's schoolbag again
like when I was 10
and I'll still be born when I'm dying
because where else do the feelings go away
if not just
deep
deep
within you?

-reborn

Lately this solitariness seems to have been
accentuated.
A shallow bowl that is being carved deeper
with every element being contained in it,
a heaviness it can't carry.
And I do not know where to place it.
For the hearth is crowded.

My poetry I desire, to be efficacious.
For if it can’t make you go to a grave to grieve
for if it can’t make you get off a plane and claim your love,
if it can’t make you humble,
deferential,
full of love,
I’ve failed.

I have a tendency to fall apart.
Emotionally,
corporeally,
objectively.
So I sleep straight and I do not move too much
and I wear pants instead of floral unconfined dresses.
I sit in the corners of café
and I hold myself together in aisle seats.
My fingers toes are unfailingly curled up.
I don't prefer being all over the place,
I am paranoid about occupying too much,
because if I do and if I break in those places,
it'll be convoluted
and they'll know just how vulnerable I am.

-limited spaces

Words fill every inch of my body.
I'm more poetry than organs I believe.
And as much as I hate carrying it all around,
I know I would feel incomplete without them.
So when I get betrayed I pick words from my heart
and when I am sick I pick words from my stomach
and when I feel weak I pick words from my knees
and when my emotions are heightened I pick words
from my eyes
and when I feel sorry I pick words from my mouth
and when I feel nothing I pick words from my soul.

-the poet's body

My gratitude has resorted to be
the strongest of my expressions.
So I apologize often and thank enough.
I fear if I lose someone,
how will I ever live
while doubting if they even forgave me.

I don't want to be just another mail in your post box,
not another passerby
who shared her umbrella on the pathway,
if I'm saving you from a stormy pour,
I hope we can drench in the heavy rains one day.

And you'll remember me as the radio will play,
and you'll tailor a raincoat only to fold it away,
because if I'm saving you from a stormy pour,
I hope we can drench in the heavy rains one day,
and you'll know you need not a cloth to save you
for I'll be here to save you over and over again.
But I hope we can drench in the heavy rains one day,
and I hope we can drench in our love one day,
and I hope we can drench...

I try to recollect and recall,
to adhere to your residual smell.
When I enter your room I touch the woods,
and smell your closet to reminisce the scent of you.
The way you would smell a little of oudh,
your favorite peanuts,
of boiled and sweetened peas
and of leather that clung to you
after hours of shattering work.
But slowly the scents are leaving your room,
just like you did.
And I do not know how to hold on.
I couldn't hold onto you after all.

-leaving

I want a love so indescribable
that'll shame Cleopatra and Mark Antony to reaffirm
their story ever existed.
I want it so alive that it'll live on even after life ceases
to exist.
I want a hand to hold in the heavens
and sway on swings of twigs.
I want the green silks to cover us in the color of love.
But if I were to not have it,
I would live in God's love.
And that too shall be unexceptional.

I want me to understand myself.
So I can introduce myself to you.
But I am confused.
What was I yesterday?
What am I today?

My body feels so heavy,
but I'm barely a few pounds,
I wonder if they ever see the heaviness around me
and not just on the scales.
What is it like to feel light?
The unconfined threads of your hair
fluttering like golden flakes
compared to the denseness of my mind.
The immaculate spark of an imminent future in your
eyes compared to the defeat of a longing in mine.
The harmonious laughter
that slowly departs from between your lips
compared to the sentimental whispers of mine.
Maybe I do know why the scales show a lesser
number,
the heaviness of a soul has no weight, does it?

-measurements

....and my father's in heaven,
and my mom's in sorrow
and I've heard home is happiness
but I don't see happiness anymore,
and I want to fly back home
but I don't see home anymore.
Where do I go?
Where do I live?
Where is home?

I am nothing without you.
You brush away the brokenness of my being
with your blemished hands.
You stroke the tangled knots of lesser meaning
through my hair.
You pick up on hope that I let slither.
You gather the resolution and walk the extra mile for
me when every step gives me a scaly feet.
I am nothing without you,
you breathe me.
Who are you, but me.
Who is me? I.

-identity

The objects that I observe
are quite suggestive at all times.
So I look at nothing like it is but what it ought to be.
The locket down my neck as the necklace of
Harmonia,
the steps up my terrace as Jacob's ladder,
the fan blades as Egils' wings.
Maybe there really is a parallel universe
where my parallel self puts into motion
all these weird imaginations that I fantasize.
But what is really better?
Reality or reverie.

I vowed of my eternal credulity
but remained indifferent to your traitorous assassin.
The melodious hymns you whispered in my ears
only clashed with the death bell you rung
underneath.
The pillows are soaked,
of water and blood
and you're long gone before the dawn.
And yet I vowed of credulity,
and am punished for being guilty.

Perhaps you didn't even recognize me.
Perhaps you didn't even know how to spell my name.
Perhaps, I was under an illusion.
And maybe our eyes didn't even meet.
But what can I do?
I already wrote a thousand poems under your name.
Maybe you'll read them one day.
But would you know it's for you?
Perhaps, never.

I knew it all this time
but I kept telling myself
it will be
it will be
it will be
and now I know it won't and yet I tell myself
it will be
it will be
it will be.
Tell me what do you call this.
Madness or cosmic reliance?

-awaiting

Hope lingers around me like grapes in a vineyard.
And I clasp each one of them
that they'll have some magical juice,
one that'll give back breath,
one that'll stop the heart attacks,
one that'll give you the power to reopen your eyes,
one that'll make you come back.
Only in the end to know
how sour the grapes were.

-losing you and hope.

You are not here to make everything right.
You might make mistakes and learn from it and try to improve but the broken vessel is not always yours to glue back. Sometimes,
just sometimes,
the universe needs your fragility to teach a strong man,
it’s okay to be soft.
It's okay to break.
Because when we crave,
we crave for a drop of water,
not the entire ocean.
Your broken pieces are valuable too.

I'm embracing hurt tonight.
I'll let it in.
I am not going to put a shield,
a safety net,
between me and the distress
that's been sitting by my roof window for some time now.
I know it's getting cold lest it gets bitter.
I'll let it slip under the quilt with me,
I’ll let it hug me,
I’ll let it sigh warmly over my icy cheeks.
I'll let it manifest its uncanny reasons
and then I’ll cry for a stranger.
I'll allow a weight to drop
from between my ribs to my stomach
and I’ll scream in my pillow.
Tomorrow morning, I will be pretentious again
and forget you were beside me.
But tonight, I’ll make bed for you.

\- the stranger in my bed

I don't know what's your favorite flower
or how do people speak of traversing the universe in love.
I'm sure there's no way of plucking stars
and naming just one of it after you seems insufficient.
I know nothing about beds of roses
or if love really is the light at the end of tunnel.
I don't really know how to love,
but if you ask me,
should I write you a poem?

- things to do in love

ENCOMIUM

The incinerating memories fade into the haze of
ambience.
I do not try to calm the expansion.
For once,
I let the fuels burn and warm my hand
against the fervor of the flames.
If at all I see,
I see ashes of resentment,
injury,
and loath.
The unruly flames howl my name.

I thought my future could be contained,
held captive in my bruise wounded hands
that still wasn't ready to let the mistakes of yesterday
slip away.
I had a notion,
what if tomorrow I'm not here,
and today my hand is just drained
of bearing this pinching feeling of yesterday
and the authority of a tomorrow
that wasn't pledged into existence.
Where is my present but in the manacles of a gone
wind
and an impending storm.
What did I do today if I wasn't even grateful.
For if I'm alive today,
it surely was yesterday's fight
and if I'll be alive tomorrow
it surely would be today's gift.
So today I'll just stand here and breathe into the
placidity.
I'll open my fist and let the weight fall.

When I walked away,
I chose myself.
And no, I'm not guilty or ashamed about it.
I'm not sorry to have shielded myself
from the neglect and the drench of harsh underlying
lies. Because when I saw my mother walking away
from societal disgrace,
I learnt.
I learnt when to choose confidence over
dependability
when I saw the disabled hands work but beg.
I learnt to choose blood over promises
when a sword was placed at my neck by a hand I
knew to be warm.
When I walked away,
I chose myself
and I never felt safer in another embrace.

Yes, I do love you.
And maybe the feeling was welcomed by me a little too late.
I failed at knowing where my own heart was.
But then one day I closed my eyes
and could tell exactly the number of curves around your smiles and the flaky snow reflecting in your dark black eyes.
I could tell how your left eye was slightly elated and that the fairness of your skin was dominated by that of your heart.
I could tell when I first saw you that I might love you but I didn't want to know.
Cause I had never met you
and yet I was so scared of losing you.
Losing the feeling of knowing you.

Life is really short;
the problem is
we've got to survive it a little longer than that.

ENCOMIUM

What's your favorite smell?
I said, "His freshly made cup of tea with the aroma of its earthen vessel."
What's your favorite place?
I said, "The hadal zone of his heart."
What's your favorite color?
I said, "The myriads of tones his unspoken scars exclaim of"
What's your favorite language?
I said, "One that speaks of our miraculous yet impending solidarity, one with the Qadr of my Lord"
What's your favorite prayer call?
I said, "One that summons me in the darkest hour of the night to beg for him.
"Who's your favorite person?
I said, "Him."

-muse

*qadr: divine intervention in human affairs

I'm relearning the hard lessons all over again.
It feels like learning to walk,
only without your watchful support.
So now that I stumble and fall,
I look for you to help me up,
only to realize
this time I've got to do it all by myself
and all over again.
My inappropriate laughs between distressing sobs
makes no sense
but how do I explain to this world
that only sees my face and not my soul
that I'm plainly trying to feel your joyful presence
that once existed and is now long gone.
I fidget and regret and confuse roads and highways,
but how do I tell
that I've lost the only correct direction of my life
to the direction of death.

I look at the dimly lit corner of my room,
there happens to be an unidentified figure
but it looks a lot like my imitated shadow.
And I wonder if the monster I'm scared of could be
me,
the deep sighs in the air, mine.
I wonder if all this while the evil I was running away
from
is named after me,
if I was the insidious threat to my subsistence.

The dust of your consciousness
is settled so thick on the shelves of your heedless concern
that any unlawful comportment
barely allows a quiver to budge you.
Where does your humanity lie?
How indifferent is your justice.
What cloth do you need to brush your inhuman mantelpiece?

-death of humanity

You don't see pain in my eyes
because it is not there.
Simple.
You think I'm going to flaunt it like an adornment in this open wide pool of unkempt secrets where you dive right in to know the reasons?
No.
It's treasured right underneath my heart
Throbbing and gasping for relief
like a fish brought out of its home
but placed safe and frozen for use later.

Your pride is not supposed to be your price.
Your pride should be the eagerness with which your knees touch the floor to pray,
your pride should be your prostration to the Lord,
your pride should be your surrender-ness for beloveds',
your pride should be your loveable propensity,
your pride should be your calm disposition,
your obliging-ness,
your endearment,
your idealization.
Your pride should be your survival
and when you'll be proud of these,
you'll see,
your substance is but of little value.

Moments I fell in love with you (and kept falling):

You stood like a piece of art with admirers around you and in a garden full of twelve hundred people, you became my masterpiece in a millisecond.

You crossed past me with your eyes affixed on the ground and on that empty driveway with lights that illuminated your face, all I could do was turn around to gaze at you till the end of our ways.

Everything you never said and everything I wish I could, slid past the little gap below the glass door that separated us and our longings. I thought the only thing that divided us in that moment was the door but I knew there was a longer way to go.

The intimacy of having recognized even your footsteps seemed to come real. I stood watching an aura from a distance, and knew it was you without having seen your face. In those later moments, that our eyes met, the space between my fantasies and reality finally receded.

I hadn't been home in a while but now that I think about it, maybe I had the wrong address all this while. I could have waited for you forever, but the moment I saw you standing

at the other end of the room, with eyes that were searching for someone familiar yet new, I knew home was where we could be built together.

Ecstasy became a definable feeling when it was felt while you sat right across, with a smile that was a little shy, and a head that kept looking my way as if wishing, how for a moment neither of us had to look anyplace else but in each other's eyes.

In every brief moment,
in every shared glimpse,
in little conversations between aisles,
I saw you,
I heard you,
and I felt you.
In every moment gone,
in every present,
in every future,
there have been moments,
there are moments,
and there'll be moments,

that I've fallen in love with you,
that I fall in love with you,
that I want to keep falling in love with you.

ENCOMIUM

The deferential heart always has one room left.
You knock at its quarters at odd hours of night
and it'll still make space for you.
That is how much it loves you.
With a crowd of thousands,
it wouldn't still spare your room for someone else.
The pictures hung on its walls startle everyone else
away,
the bed sheets beckon you home.
All you need to do,
is come back.

I'm touch starved,
not in the sense of communicating corporeally,
but rather a much deeper actuality.
I want to feel animate and dynamic.
I want a vigorous gush of howling breeze to shake me
off the ground and shriek of a worthwhile existence
that I've been stone deaf against.
I don't want erotic tangibility
but just someone to simply hold on to my hand
between the two of theirs
and clench it taut enough and long enough
for me to realize I'm still human
and I can still feel.
And you see,
that's how dead I am.

-allow me to feel

ICU

Will these blue nights linger on for forever,
will I still keep my auditory senses into instant reaction
even when there's no sign of a ringing bell tonight.
Should I still spread a sheet on the edge of the door
and lay there like a fetus waiting for you to call me
even when I know you're not in the room.
The smell of remedies still abides by between the wall of a healing chart and the rusting cylinders that have left marks
on the floor of my begging prayers.
The drips of consciousness hang above the bed from
a syringe but it too fails to find its area of reaction.
The last minute you were just here
and now it's just the unsterilized pain.
Your cure calls you,
come back maybe?

A sad world.
I live in a sad world.
Where to be verbal means to be offensive.
Where to care means to hurt yourself.
Where demanding love means demanding authority.
Where to be opinioned means to abuse.
Where to cry means to be dramatic.
Where to joke means to mock.
Where being you is not being you.

- essay from a 14 year old

To the one who fell out of love with me
I hope it didn't take much of you
I hope it wasn't a tribulation
there's less to love of me through my insides and outsides
I now keep myself mundane to keep you away from me
I want you to have the gateau
for I could only ever be the candle you blow and discard.

Permit me, I would name my poems after you.
The words I inscribe scream of you.
In pain,
in love,
in longing,
in loss.

But you're an artist, you can do it.
And they do not hesitate to ask for your help.
For words in our brain are tangibly free
and we're here to create.
Yet are we once asked as creators,
how intense an emotion do we feel
to create something flawlessly beautiful
out of flawed broken hearts.

-to the artists

Devotedness is a fable
and its tale has been recited down through centuries.
There will repeatedly be someone better in your life through every interim.
But tell me, can I keep my fingers crossed
that you'll find your salvation in the ruins of my being?
Tell me if you'll live by the myth of finding sufficiency in me.

-am I enough?

I'm like that background noise,
the harp that's rarely required by the orchestra.
The person who walks behind you like a shadow
but has no recognition.
I'm the backstage that gets no coverage
and is always in the shambles to let you put a good
show in front.
The preamble that never got to become a segment of
the main plot.
I'm the memory that was never written down to
cherish.
The mosaic that was broken but never beautiful.
And I'm learning that in the relay
of completing and complimenting another soul,
I've been me
and not myself at all.

Perhaps this pain isn't mine.
Perhaps it belongs to someone else.
Perhaps I'm chosen to bear it in the interest of that someone. Perhaps that someone needs me to.
Perhaps I'm the instrument for the melody of their life.
Then should I give up?
Or should I bear this a little while longer?

-bearer for you

Ibn 'Umar said,
"Servant of Allah, what will your name be
tomorrow?"

Which is to say,
what am I today,
what am I right now,
what will I be tomorrow?
A human today, breathing right now, corpse
tomorrow? Corporeal today, struggling right now,
silent tomorrow?
A population today, contributing right now, ash
tomorrow?
A name today, a meaning right now, a memory
tomorrow?

-in a split second

ENCOMIUM

If you walk up to me and offer to buy me a drink,
I'll be a little surprised
and then shake my head to deny the offer.
Then I'll tell you stories of dolor and an abode far unseen,
of translucent dreams and unsubjugated womanliness,
of plenty rooms in an abandoned kingdom
and an everlasting summer of goodbyes.
Our glasses shall condense and remain untouched
but if you offer to buy me a drink,
you'll be the one drunk.

DAD

How I hold onto grief:

I wear your T-shirt's that drown me and clench them to my chest/ read the little stories you wrote while you were sick/ touch your pillow as if you slept here last night/ try to discover little notes and used tissues from the insides of your blazer/ wear your cap in the winter weather to feel your long gone warmth/ spray your oudh all around the room to reminisce your heavenly odour/ sniff your handkerchiefs that hold the sweats of your endeavor/ wear your watch to make you exist in this time again.

ENCOMIUM

You ask me
why do I always feel obliged
to fix all that's wrong and broken
and then rupture the spine of my existence.
I'm left obliging
and fixing again.

ENCOMIUM

You need to move aside
if you are to quiver when the mountain shakes,
and the volcanos erupt.
You need to dig your feet deeper in sand
if you believe that the tides are going to take you away.
You need to guard yourself,
protect every inch from the hurting rays of the sun and shards
that might crack every vulnerable part of you.
And you need to know a woman is all of it.
Not just a rustling wind that sings melodies in the ear,
but a swallowing ocean that can consume the earth
as easily as tossing the shells across the shore.
You need to know
that she could be as gentle and kind a feather,
a building held on foundations that might break for once,
but she's also a resting growing forest,
that burns but doesn't leave its roots,
that knows her beauty is too objective a resort for fantasy,
but her power is a hell fire,
begged to be saved from.

-alnisa|woman

I'm exhausted of my own arguments.
Tired of my own contradictions.
Drained of my own poetry.
How it's always running between dreams and war,
between death and immorality,
between apocalypse and identity.
How it's never just about one thing,
one person,
one life,
one suffering.
How it's so misleading.
Makes me wonder
if I do not recognize singularity,
how will I become one?
What should I be?
Multitudes or particular.

I’m afraid that if you leave,
you’ll take parts of me away with you.
The humble softer one,
the generous grateful one,
the sensitive hopeful one,
the spirited loving one.
You’ll take away the part of me
that wakes up with gentleness on her mouth
and a recitation of shukr on her tongue,
the part which wants to stay alive
even with an unidentified purpose,
the part that doesn’t mind getting drenched
as long as the chai you make for me shall make me
warm,
the part that wants to draw sunrises and sunsets for
you
on days that it’s cloudy.
I take your name after every breath
to make you a part of me,
but when you’ll be gone,
no part of me shall be left.

-don’t leave.

*shukr: gratitude

The graveyards are filled with rotting bouquets
and letters that are blown from one to another's
burial bed.
Of deafening silences
and wishes of one last conversation.
While we are still here,
would you promise me togetherness in the heaven?

-al-firdaws

ENCOMIUM

I want you to think of me when you read someone's
poem in the most beautiful handwriting.
When you see a white rose wilting on your coffee
table.
When someone smiles at you with the dimples on
their cheek, I want you to think of my crooked little
tooth.
When you search for meanings in the dictionary,
I want you think of the way we found out meanings
in each other.
I want you to think of me while making promises,
and when the sky is clear and has no moon.
I want you to think of me,
but not as a lost baggage or as an obligation,
not as a heartache or a grief around your neck,
not as a house who couldn't shelter you from the
thunderstorms
or as a city ending in ruins.
I want you to think of me for as long as you feel
you can still love the damaged undeserving parts of
me,
for as long as thinking of me doesn't hurt you,
but the moment I become anything else
other than a memory full of warmth,
please forget me.

The jingling of the keys will scare you
but you will still unlock the door.
Confessing will frighten you
but you'll still gather the courage.
The bright light will blind you
but you'll still leave the darkness behind.
Loving someone will chill your blood
but you'll still wrap your arms around it.
And that's what your gallantry should be,
that's how voracious your appetite for power should
be. Nothing should stop you,
not even your own horror.

-manifest

You make promises of memories,
but you fail to show up at my doorsteps.
You make itineraries for future visits,
but fail to sit beside me for a remember-able moment.
You talk about a succeeding life,
but you’re somehow missing right now.
How is it that you’re so much a part of my future
but I’m forgetting you in my present.

-right now

I'm in need, you're sufficient. There's a difference.
I'm an end and you're its beginning. There's a difference.
I'm the unease and you're their pride. There's a difference. There's a distance.
And I'm not sure
I can traverse the path correctly
to reach you.

-change

12
9
3
6

I can't sleep.
I drink a lot of caffeine and tell my friends I know it's bad
but I don't stop.
I don't want to sleep.
At 2am, I cook myself some Shepherd's pie
and freeze it back at 3am.
It feels weird having it without you.
At 3:30, I hallucinate you sitting next to me and talking to me about the coldest hours of night you've survived
and at 4:00 you leave me in mine.
At 4:30, I pray a silent prayer
and whisper to Him in prostration,
at 5:00 I dry out my eyes.
At 5:30 I re-read old conversations of you telling me to sleep because it's very late
and at 6:00 I wish I slept forever right next to your ground.

-qabr

And then I saw you and you smiled
like the poem I've been trying to write about
since nights innumerable.
A little broken but a lot more beautiful.
A little indecipherable but a lot more reassuring.
A little beyond expression but a lot more hidden.
And a little unread but a lot more seen.

My sorrow has numerous names.
Some are antonyms to feelings of ecstasy and elation
and others are synonyms with the very purpose of
my existence.
One sounds like the call of help in a beggar's mouth
while another like the chants of Allah from
dervishes.
One sounds like a prayer of forgiveness
while other of looming miseries.
One sounds like a sweet cry
while the other
sounds like my name.

-names

I clench all the heartbreaks I've gathered for so long
and sit right in the middle of a waterless pool
wishing someone would put down the hose
and drown me with all my grief.
But when they find my body
will they pick up the heartbreaks and bury them with
me too? How long am I supposed to carry this
misery?
Is this life not sufficient?

I tried seeing home for what it's meant to be.
A safe resort,
mom's delicacies,
dad's loud laughs and warm hugs when he returns from work. But who decides what's home meant to be.
For I still have it
but only without any of these things.
It's locked and empty and the furniture has gathered dust.
I don't know if it's safe or not, but I'm not.
I don't know if the refrigerator still has a rotten delicacy from her last cook,
but I know I'm hungry.
And I don't know,
or maybe I do,
that it's certainly lacking of his laugh and warmth
and I know that I'm decaying
just like my home.

- definitions

I believe we are all mansions in ourselves.
With extensive gardens that are roamed around for its beauty, water fountains that are refreshing to another's soul,
a gourmet kitchen that serves empathy and mercy in gold platters,
a study that notes everyone's travails but their own
and then a little room
on the far-far outskirts near the boundary
where the real,
bare soul sits
and waits for someone
who won't be just another guest of the mansion's grandeur.

I traced the path of a love left halfway
and found its destination to be a bright light.
Which is to say-
its fine if sometimes you've got to take a longer route
and stay on it even when time feels stuck.
It's fine to prostrate on that prayer mat five times a
day
and repeat the same supplication over and over again
even when it isn't being answered instantly.
It's fine to feel that the wait is draining you of your
patience. Its fine to feel a little lost and a little alone.
For when your time will eventually come,
when He will finally grant your prayers,
when patience will feel renewed and replenished
and when you'll finally reach the bright light,
you'll know that the path of love was never
unguided.
You'll know that the remaining half way
awaited your footsteps.

Will I be there for me when I need me?
When I cry
will I reassure myself of a better time?
When I need to feel love
will I open my arms to hug myself?
When I need someone to talk
will I be a safe listener and keeper?
When I'll accidentally slit my finger with a blade
will I leave it unattended or resort to its aid?
When I prick my foot with a thorn
will I shush the little cry
or will I accept that it's okay to express?
When I need to be the person I have been to
everyone else, will I be there for me?
And if not,
who will?

-on loving yourself

I don't know for how long will writing about it all,
be a substitute to feeling it any less.
I don't know if these words are any more worthy
than cornered residue.
Or if any of this is actually healing me
like it is meant to and exclaimed
by poets, artists, musicians, lovers.
I don't even know if you actually meant something to
me
or if I was simply trying to mean something to
myself, someone worthy of being loved,
someone worthy of being just a mere unpronounced
name.
I also do not know of reciprocation or resonation
but maybe a little of separation.
And I surely do not know how to end this poem,
but I'm only trying to heal by the end of it
without even beginning.

When on some days I wake up and decide to love myself,
I do not write.
I make chai for two just to be a little less lonely.
I walk as if on piano tunes
so my soul wouldn't feel dragged on.
I stand on rooftops even during pitiless sunshine
and allow myself to breathe the way I would if it were raining. On days I decide to love myself,
I try to not care so I can protect myself.
I empathize with my own grief so that tomorrow I wouldn't need anyone to sympathize with me.
I become less observant,
inattentive,
afar from the broken mirrors.
On days I decide to love myself,
I just try to hurt myself a little less.

-a little less

My grief has become opposing to my actions.
So I want to hear your voice so bad
but cannot make myself plug into your audios.
I want to talk to you so bad
that I never open our little conversations.
It's like having all your habits and behaviors and
manners that I inherited but hating myself everyday
more and more for what I'm becoming.
It's like having your first name as my middle name,
but not wanting to respond when anyone calls.
So when my grief tells me to feel your presence as if
you're right here,
I instead break down to think
how encompassing your absence is.

The day I cut my thumb with a knife
and was scared that someone would see the band aid
is the day I realized how insecure of self-care am I.
How hard is it in this world to love yourself first,
to prioritize yourself,
to set apart your own meal,
to breathe across the ocean without feeling the guilt of someone else's captivity,
to protect yourself from the storm before offering the umbrella to someone else,
to hold safe the key of your happiness without worrying about how others have a jammed door.
To care is to be humble, I know.
But how hard is it to be humble to yourself for once?

Things I actually enjoy while carrying sadness around in my eyes:

Sitting in group therapy sessions and seeing people heal/ a downpour so heavy that it floods the desires of the heart/ a daughter dancing with her father/ being so giving and sharing even while being empty/ living on little means today while dying for everything tomorrow.

Do not neglect the love of two.
That of a poet and that of a person on a prayer mat.
For the poet, immortalizes you
while the forehead in prostration asks for his life span
to be added to yours.
For one, writes you poems
and the other looks at you like you're poetry of the
finest Gulzar Faiz Ghalib.
For one, sings of your memories
and the other memorizes you like a surah
and for one finds your presence in his art
and the other circumambulates the Kaaba begging
and praying to bring an end to your absence in his
life.

How my scream sounds like:

The anechoic chamber/ the smoothest winds during
twilight / the hiss created by the agitation of the
eardrums / the breath of a claustrophobic person in
the tiniest space / the foam on the beach touching
my feet / the crying of a failed man at his lover's
funeral/ zero decibels.

- scream in silence

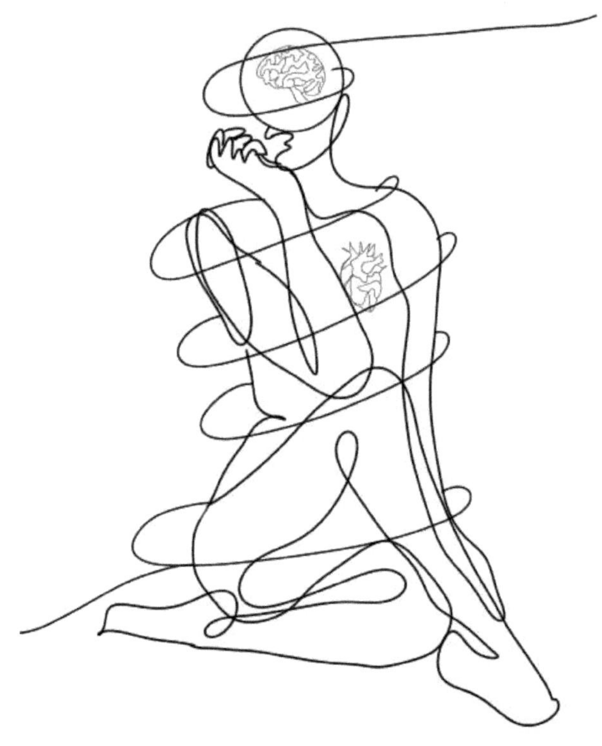

Sometimes I wish my own body would devour me,
turn my outsides in and drown me in the thirty
percent water and thirty percent tears that it is.
Because I feel my heartbeat in my ears,
under my foot,
on the nerves on my forehead.
I feel it everywhere but in my heart.
Because there are days my ribs feel so broken,
that every element of it seems like they're floating
with the
miseries inside of me.
And my eyes change colors,
but not that of rainbows
instead of thunderstorms.
If I hold my wrist too tight for too long,
or pinch myself sharply,
there's no mark left and it only feels numb.
Oh how I wish I could stay inside of my own body
and not outside.
How I wish I could hide inside of my own body
without a face or name,
for no one else can possibly keep me
and my hurt.

You cannot only let home be where it doesn't hurt,
clawing at the soft meat
only after it was butchered and washed.
When it floods,
you need to know that your home,
the safest spot,
drowns too.
And the gardens,
lanes,
lamps of your street
will no more have the same addresses.
And when you'll stand at the doors,
your home will beckon you to run away.
But don't.
Come to a halt and tell your home
that it's okay if it's not warm at the moment,
and if the cemented walls are wet to lean on,
tell your home that it's okay if the flour sack is empty
for your heart is too,
and then sit with your home and learn the survival
tricks and try to feel whole with it,
try to heal your home of the hurt
and heal along.

ENCOMIUM

You tell me I have so many faces, as if that is cruelty.
I tell you yes, I look like everyone who left me.
That's all they left behind, a resemblance.
And that is why I look
a little enthralling
a little exciting
a little broken
a little needy.
And today,
I look like that childhood best friend whose manners
were polite but heart got a little bitter with time.
Yesterday,
I looked like someone who needed me but for whom
I had nothing to offer,
so I looked betrayed.
And tomorrow,
I might try to look a little like myself all alone.
So tomorrow,
you'll see death and blue blood running down my
nerves
and a grieving
despairing
dispirited skeleton.
And then I'll ask you
if it's still one face that's admirable to you.

When I look at you I see what might have made
God's creation so sublime.
I have watched sunsets and sunrises,
tides and births,
emeralds onyx beryl,
Baghdad Gaza Kashmir,
Seven Wonders of the World,
the lost treasures,
my beloved, I have watched God's most beautiful
creation, woman of this world.
But when I look at you,
everything else seems like a ruin,
and I know even if I were to see the Garden of Eden,
your blossoming heart would be par excellence
for it would make mountains bow
and angels shade their wings,
and I wouldn't know Saturn ever existed.

-your beauty

ENCOMIUM

When your shoe gets torn,
you take it to the cobbler.
When your robe gets frayed,
you take it to the tailor
and when your watch gets shattered,
you take it to the horologist.
So when your heart gets broken,
you're supposed to take it your lord.
He mends the soul,
he stitches the wound
and he calms the ticking palpitations.
He fixes you beautifully
for he is the sole creator.

GRIEF
SUN MON TUE WED THU FRI SAT
1 2 3 4 5 6
7 8 9 10 11 12 13
14 15 16 17 18 19 20
21 22 23 24 25 26 27
28 29 30

ENCOMIUM

Giving a date to grief, is like marking it on a calendar
and telling yourself that this is the day you do
nothing but cry.
This day you're allowed to,
but on other days, you need to forget.
Remembering it on the same day every year is a
defense mechanism just so that I can blame the day
for it,
and put red crosses.
My consciousness tells me,
"you can put it down, let it go,
you don't have to carry it around with you."
The grief,
the loss,
the longing.
I ask, put it down where?
On the calendar that will come around every year
or the grave where there's already so much pain?
Where do I put it down?
When it's carved into the very certainty of
my past
present
and future.

- 11.07.21

This is me
telling the ones who read this poetry
everything that I instead want to tell you:

your rhapsodic eyes is what I write poems on/ when I see an end to something, I hope it's replaced with the beginning of you / my conversations revolve around you and your voice that I still don't know the sound of/ when I hope for God's willingness, I wish it to be for us / when I think of a miracle, I thank the universe for your birth/ when I prepare for the hereafter, I prepare so I can be in it with you.

ENCOMIUM

The destiny of my love is directed towards wherever
your shadow falls.
It has no consistency on the compass,
but has stayed the same in my heart since I've ever
known you.
And I turn towards you on days of Eid
so my soul could celebrate,
and my heart humbly bows down towards you
on days I have shukr in my heart,
I cry in sajdah
on days I wish you would be that one miracle of my
life,
and I chant your name before dusk and dawn.
They say your truest love has to be that with your
Rabb,
I say while finding love with my Rabb,
he gave me you.

*sajdah: prostration

I'll teach my daughter how to fall out of love before
falling in. I'll tell her, it's necessary and it's gruesome.
On days she weeps into a pillow,
I'll make her count those tears
so she can multiply it for the happiness she deserves.
When she'll fear disregard,
I'll show her that the only validation she needs
is of the person staring back from the mirror.
And on days, she'll think she is incapable of building
a home, I'll make sure she knows
that her heart has the widest residence.
I'll tell my daughter,
as long as she has love in her heart,
she has love around her,
because on most days we teach ourselves what love
is,
but fail to understand what love isn't.

-daughters who deserve love

ENCOMIUM

We write of odes, and sunshine eyes,
of poetries, and men to cry,
how dreams become cold and knowledge unsafe,
tucked under the bed in a broken crate.
Of evenings at home and whiskey in saucers,
of raging windstorms looking like daughters.
We write of bitter lies,
it looks like the face of artists,
of shards of glass,
they lie distorted.
We write of everything but mostly nothing at all,
for we fail to write our own faults.

My last voice message:
Today once again, you picked up your phone to call me
but the call went straight on voice mail,
the receiver on this end has no name anymore.
I did though,
a very precious name,
when I was alive and living and loving.
But by the time you'll hear this
I'll be called a body.
I recorded this last message to finally say it to you.
Tell you that I'm tired,
the sun doesn't shine down on me anymore
and the trays of food at my bedside table
is going stale lying here for days.
Something is pulling me up towards the sky
but also deep down into the earth
and so I'm being stretched on both ends and tearing apart.
No one asked me to say this out aloud,
no one cared much
but I haven't slept in weeks
and so if I could sleep for an eternity,
I'd love to.

Empty bottles of pills lie around me like herds of
sheep in a meadow.

And there's no one to clear them up.
Which is to say,
I'm starting to look like a dumping ground.
I have newspapers on every window
so no one would see me
or they really would throw dirt in.
I prepared a black suit
so they would dress me up for my funeral
but I think you'll find me lying in a blood stained
white sheet. Maybe you can bury me in your pity and
sympathies.
My doors are unlocked so you can come in.
But before you leave,
please clear this voicemail.

-on quitting

I have my mother's tenderness in the way I love
and my father's resistance in the way I can avoid
expression of my love.
I know which wire is to be joint where,
and when to wash my hands before wiping off my
tears after I've touched a jar of spices.
I have my mother's strength by which I'm still passing
every second of everyday without the one man in
both of our lives that we loved
and I have my father's memories and promises to
keep us both alive.
I know when to fear death,
and I know how to hold onto hope even when dying.

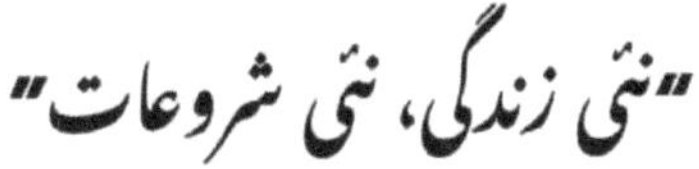

I have my father's last words
hinged to every letter of my poetry
and I have my mother's language to write it in.
Together I bring them on paper,
so they're here with me forever.

*Urdu translation:
new life, new beginning

I’m exhausted of this embodiment.
I’m tired of being a human.
I want to be a poem,
written by the hands of a poet
who can structure me with rhymes and rhythms.
Maybe I can look a little like Croatia,
with the mouth of a heavenly creature gasping for union.
Or maybe like Greece,
with a lady lying on her bed,
her hair tied up while her pillow soaks her tears.
I want to look beautiful,
like a fantasy,
a pearl dug out after pulling shovels across the mind.
I want to be anything and anyone
but myself right now.

Li- Young Lee said, I've been lonely for you.
Which is to say,
my longing has its place in an affectionate corner of
the garden where I saw you first,
but my loneliness for you has been encompassing my
home. From the dining room table to the pashmina in
the trunk, every particle of existence awaits your
presence.
I disconnect my telephone
because your voice rings around in my corridors.
When I think of you,
something within me pulls me inside
as if to say, stay back.
Don't be the victim to a ghost.
How do I tell them,
I'm the one dying.

-longings

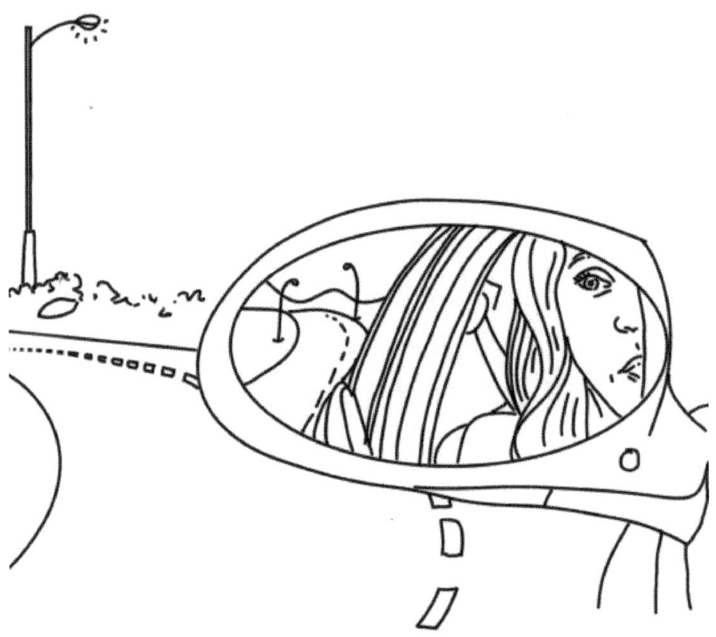

On the 25th of August,
I crossed the same lane again that
screamed of hidden horrors and unidentified victims.
I reach for my phone and put you on emergency call,
impulsively so, like I did last time.
It struck me only when I saw the last lamp post
flickering and dying, that you’re dead too.
My only hope,
my only light,
my only call,
had no receiver on the other end.
So when someone asks me why I don’t sit on the
passenger seat anymore,
I tell them I’m scared.
The long drives were only safe with you
and now every road and street has harsh fatal
potholes
and men looking at me through their rear view
mirror.
I still haven’t learnt driving dad,
and the steering wheel of my life has no control.
And do you think it’s fine
if I wish this was my last ride back home?

ENCOMIUM

On some days, I die a little and you need to let me.
I see the end closely lying on my couch, a white rug
drawn over me, so if I did die,
I would be in the color of the shroud already.
Those some days I still write poetry but not about
mahtab
mulaqat
moujza
but about
qayaamat
ranjish
and a longing for Jannah.
I don't put my sunflowers, tulips and roses into a
water jar
but I let it wilt like me.
Maybe you can put them between pages of my
books?
On some other day,
when I do die,
put me between the pages of your past life
and allow me to disappear.
But please,
water my sunflowers.

*mahtab: moonlight / mulaqat: meeting / moujza: meeting / qayaamat: last day / ranjish: resentment / jannah: heaven

ENCOMIUM

I'll give time a little time,
I'll not check the calendars,
I'll put down the clocks.
I'll throw the watches in the lake
and I'll not check to see if the sun has set.
I'll let the tea boil and spill and drink of what's left,
I'll hang the clothes and let it get drenched with rain
before it finally dries on the third day,
I'll forget I ever planted a seed and come back 20
years later to see it bearing fruits.
I'll love you now
but I'll give time a little time
until its right
and then I'll ask time to pause
the moment you are here.

Today, there is no guarantee of us.
But tomorrow, it shall be better.
Maybe tomorrow there still won't be a guarantee of us,
but we'll try to stick up with each other.
On days, we shall be unsure of our fates,
we'll make sure we love each other in the present moment and on days we'll hope we end up together,
we'll remind each other of the khair in this postponement. Maybe someday we'll finally be able to say what we feel,
even though our rusting heart is aware of our affection,
maybe our book of fate was written long before our existence, but maybe tomorrow,
even God will make an exception.

-fates

*Khair: goodness

I visit the beach with my sadness.
I lay down with it on the sand that feels as boiling as that of hell but I know it isn't.
I don't tell my sadness that you'll get over it
or that it is in your head,
I don't tell it to stop scrapping its skin off from what gave it burns.
I let it feel the warmth of the sand
and wait until the foamy frothy cold water reaches to cool it down.
Then we jump up to take a dip,
we throw the calmness of the water on each other
to settle our turbulences,
we hold each other's hand
so the mighty waves do not take us away,
and I kiss it on its forehead.
We build sandcastles
and name it after our most beloved person.
My sadness named it after me.
So when the water broke it down,
my sadness finally did let go of me.

Jat khalisat: your place is empty.
Which is to say,
your seat at the dining table has not been sat on
since you left, the car is sold off after it lost its most
swift driver,
the beret still hangs from the hook with little strands
of your hair crossed with its thread.
The diary has had no entry since 12th of July,
the spectacles still have the droplets of your tears
and your crisply ironed white shirt still lies folded.
Your name derives no response
and the place you left empty will never be filled.

-spaces

You think my brown eyes are a little hurt
and I think your smile is a little painful.
You think my shivering hands have held the heaviest burdens and I think your weak shoulders have carried everyone's pain. You think my cracked ankles have stood brutalities of time
and I think your knees are bent not because you lost but because you were humbled.
You think my heart has housed every passing stranger
and I think your words have healed every fallen leaf.
You think I want you,
I know I need you.

-impressions

I wish holding onto my hope was paid by the hour
because I'm struggling my way through it.
I wake up every morning,
put on my suit of patience,
brush away the contemplations of the night,
wash the dirt of my failed past,
tie strength into the breaking strands of my hair
and stuff my insecurities,
discomposure
and a handkerchief of sweating unease
into my bag.
The moment I step out,
all I look like is a leaf hanging from the twisted part
of its stem. Trying not to fall apart,
trying not to fall down.

If the world were to split right now,
I would be fine with it.
If this would be the end and the last night where my pillow gets drenched,
I would be fine with it.
For I have endured and I have had patience
and while I have longed for you and waited for you
to finally complete what they call the half of me,
your absence has actually been more encompassing.
After all, the need of the heart is to be thoroughly filled, whether it be with acceptance or with longing.
And once it's filled,
its purpose is served.

Descriptions of my heart:

A filthy soft toy in the hands of a poor kid/ the lost coin to buy bun from after which there's no food for survival/ the broken buttons down the laboring man's shirt/ the hole in a wall that shows another world / the packed suitcases leaving a war torn land / the lost love letter from the mailbox / a leaf that detached and flew to a never existing universe.

It's already November
and I don't know how much longer I can love you.
The trees are shedding leaves and they bleed red,
my heart is holding onto the last of you.
It's already November,
my feet are cold in all seasons
but today they're numb too,
how much longer do I wait for the warmth.
The rains come and go,
they are unsure of their site,
but you know when you have to come home, right?
It's already November,
will you be home in December?

-the months that await you

To not be the most beautiful person in the world,
not be someone that can be fallen for at first sight,
and still love someone
is like sitting on the edge on a broken bridge,
hoping, just hoping
that it won't crack open beneath you.
It's like telling someone that my heart beats only for you,
but I understand if I am not what your dreams look like.
It's like taking a lock,
tying a thread of prayers around it
and dropping it into a wishing well,
but no one has the keys to it even if found.
It's like my love can be a substitute for sunsets on evenings that it rains,
but I'll not always be pretty.
It's like flipping a coin but neither of the sides are in my favor,
like the odds were never mine.
It's like wishing for a moment that I'll be loved back,
but hoping they won't ever see my face.

-insecurities

When you shook hands with me,
you left a patch of emptiness on the very palm where
I search for lines that'll make us meet,
where intersections feel like they're making the initial
letters of your name.
The same palms that take the shape of a begging
bowl
just so that a drop of mercy will fill it to its brim.
The patch of emptiness has felt nothing else since.
It has held taut the warmth of your caress,
And the nerves linking it to my heart,
beckons you back.

-that one handshake

ENCOMIUM

In my attempts between trying to learn the sound of
your name to that of trying to forget your existence,
I've finally allowed myself to breathe.
A breath that isn't weighted by the ugly scars that
you gave, nor another tear shed because of you.
I still cry and feel every little inch of pain that my
body summons to,
but I allow it only so that it can heal.
I collect every tear
and throw in into the salty vastness of the oceans,
a place from where I don't have to care where they
flow.
A place that isn't yours anymore.
So while I clear out everything that belonged to you,
I hold myself back
because I was never yours.

ENCOMIUM

I have written a lot of poems
for people whose eyes I haven't looked into
or whose hug I don't know what feels like.
The fabrication of words into compound sentences
using every possible language rule is easier and
simpler when you're only writing out of imagination,
out of what your mind has created.
But how do I write a poem for someone that I truly
love? Someone who is real and not a product of my
poetry.
For their eyes are indescribable,
their smile drops honey that cannot be contained,
and I don't know how long I want to be in the
embrace of their hug.
Someone whom I want to share the last cup of chai
with every day,
and stop playing songs because their voice is what I
want to hear.
How do I write about someone whose existence in
themselves is like a poem written by God,
my dear,
how do I write a poem for someone like you?

Let's create a language and call it our own.
Let's share every goodbye,
every complain,
every confession in it.
Let's call it complete,
call it immaculate,
even if sometimes it'll fail to say everything.
Let this language of ours hold us together
on days that our hands can't,
let it translate everything I say into poetry
for your ears to hear.
Let this language remain silent,
let it be like peace on our tongues,
let it rest.
Let this be unknown to all,
starve in other's presence,
settle in its own unconsciousness.
Let this language be only ours,
let it perish with the end of us.

Go, save yourself from me.
Do not ignite the candles
and sit on the other end of the table with me,
do not eat all that I cooked for you with less of oil
and more of my love,
do not wait for me outside while it rains
or hold the door of your car and heart open for me,
do not walk me home when it's late at night,
do not put the coats on the hook for me,
do not put on the bonfire and warm me with your
touch.
Do not open the windows to let the air in when I
suffocate,
do not put out your cigarette to keep me safe,
do not read letters from 1999
and do not stay back just for me.
Because if you did,
you'll know I'm just another intoxication,
and darling you should know your cigarettes are safer
than me. You should know your love doesn't look like
me.

Being sad but happy in the same moment:

gazing at the Noor of mom's face but being petrified of losing her one day too/ laughing at jokes and picking up cookie crumbs that your friends dropped but shedding a drop of tear on the floor knowing they'll not hang around forever/ staring at the clock being thankful for your presence in this beautiful time but recalling what happened exactly at this time last year/ renovating your house putting up golden pieces of art but hurting because these halls will never be walked down again by someone that once stayed in there/ having innumerable people around to love you but not the one that your heart has loved.

Make me your home.
Put a braided brown mat at my door
and drop every tear soaked cloth on it before you enter.
Make me five stories tall and at every floor,
leave your agony,
apprehension,
anxiety,
affliction,
and ailments.
When the walls of my kitchen turn black,
put on a little chimney and allow the burning smokes of a roasted bloating wound be taken far away from us.
Let the corridors be dimly lit,
just enough to tell you that the light you're looking for,
will always be in here waiting for you.
Light some sweet scented candles on the brim of my balcony and allow yourself to reclaim the strength from it.
Whisper your grievous tales,
for these walls of your home have ears
and let the windows remain unbolted at night

so I can let every sorrow of yours escape.
Make me your home and make me on a sea side,

so on days I get
suffocating
strangling
stifling,
you can go out and breathe a little.
But if you make me a home,
please,
do not abandon me.

-human home

THINGS
ABBU
TAUGHT
ME

I learnt from my dad how to live even without what
you love, to never keep my keys in a bunch
so if one is lost I'll have another,
to save woods for night when winters are haunting,
to boil the tea twice before serving,
to let the guests choose the amount of sugar,
to remember where I come from and what my
destination should be,
to believe I can have the power over everything I see.
I learnt to believe in the hereafter,
for that is the place he resides in now,
I learnt to pray and beg for Jannah,
because that is where he peacefully sleeps now.
I learnt from my dad to hold a hand out to my past,
let it live in the present with me,
I learnt to hold my agony in my arms,
caress it and allow it to break with me.
I learnt hope is mightier than the death that took him
away, only in this moment I have to ask it to stay,
I have to know how to mold my pain into usefulness,
I have learnt from my dad all that you hear me say.

ENCOMIUM

I lean against metro doors
knowing they are going to open through
and sit at the edge of the highest towers
watching life run under me
and I cross highways without looking up for once
but I swear I'm not trying to die.
I'm only trying to feel something,
anything,
that'll tell me I'm still alive.
I'm only trying to suffer a little
so I know I still have the courage to fight it.
I'm only trying to slit an incision on my body
so I know I'm not turning blue.
I'm only trying to allow the loss to breed in my bones,
so I know that I have to find sufficiency within myself.
I swear my love I'm not trying to die,
I'm only trying to know if I can still survive.

ENCOMIUM

Being in love is like standing under the most
scorching sun in mid-July on a high tide day across
the shore while the sand burns you and still, not
wanting to flinch a bit because in that moment every
element of nature seems to be embracing you in its
warmest tenderness.
It's like waking up every day and seeing another page
of your incomplete book being benevolently hand
written so you can read it to sleep the forthcoming
night.
Being in love is like having a pocket full of keys but
knowing that you won't need them because every
door of another's heart has been left open wide for
you.
It's like being in conversation with a listener
who is perpetually, unceasingly, earnestly
listening to every unsaid
undervalued
unbound
thought of yours.
Being in love dear is so subtly
obsessively
intoxicatingly
being with you,
only you.

I kept all my trauma in that one little finger of mine
and then it accidentally got stuck on the door of your house. So while I bled,
but never shed a tear or screamed out loud
in the fear that you'll know I'm hurting,
I actually allowed some of it to drop on the welcome mat on your porch.
Maybe tomorrow when you'll sit on the stairs above it,
while laughing out loud with someone that you love,
watching the stars fall
and forgetting every pain you've ever felt,
it will slide out from under the mat
and step down the stairs.
It will smile at you for it'll recognize you
but it'll try its best to remain invisible
like just I was to you at times.
Then it will slowly exit your driveway
but not come back to me,
maybe then my pain will finally find its path away from the both of us,
for my little finger cannot shelter it anymore.

-letting go

I look at myself and feel like Van Gogh's last rough
draft before the canvas rolls had its marvelous feat of
The Starry Night.
What difference could there be
except I'm a scorching sun instead of a yellow moon
light,
a stroke of black instead of the attention grabbing
blue sky. What difference could there be
except I never made it to the museum of arts
but laid in fields under bags of husk,
gathering dust.
What difference
except I'm a little devoid of meaning and significance
rather than an emotion evoking piece of work.
What difference,
except the biggest,
the mightiest,
that I can never be the master piece itself?

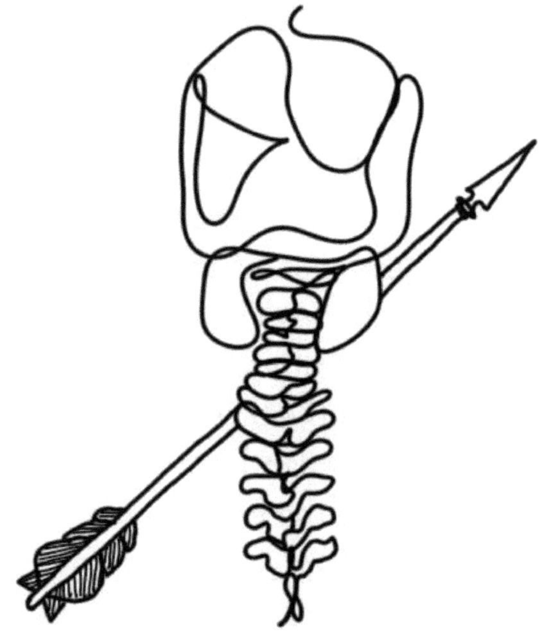

ENCOMIUM

I try to love like I've never been hurt.
With a softness that if you were pointing arrows at me,
I'll offer you my spine to enjoy your aim.
I would smile at you, and be glad that out of everyone you could have chosen to break,
you chose me.
I focus only on the fact that you chose me.
I try to hold my heart in my chest so that it will keep beating for you, but I know the moment you ask me to take it out and hand it over,
I'll do it and die for it.
I love with the kind of ferociousness
that I'll let my nerves pound and my soul jitter
out of the longing that I succumb to while waiting for you,
but in the moment you'll want to be reassured from your own doubts,
I will offer every speck of hope and peace
and ask you to just wait a little longer
while my own existence draws out.
I love,
not because I want love but because for once,
I want to feel what love is like,
because for once I want to know that I'm capable of love.

Suddenly you were right there.
Suddenly you were not just a dream,
a hope,
a longing.
I held your hand for the first time ever,
and it didn't feel unfamiliar.
In that brief moment
I so badly wanted to believe that now that I've held you once,
I can hold you forever.
And maybe, in my heart I finally did.
In my heart,
your name was written a thousand times over,
and my mind fought every negative connotation to what disastrous a fate we could lead ourselves into,
but to believe,
to believe and hope and pray and wait was all I had,
was all I wanted.
To have your love,
to have you forever,
to have you after several trials and tribulations
only came later,
only came more beautiful than thought of.

ENCOMIUM

Maybe this is a poem,
or maybe everything that you read here
are just some very fabricated alluring pieces of words
sewn together that yearn and hurt
and are in war with themselves.
Maybe this trivial, trifling compilation
of non-rhythmic, unstructured sentences
are merely some uncomfortable screams of mine
that couldn't find its place in immoderate laughter.
Maybe this one time this piece will not depict perfection
but confusion,
chaos
and complication.
Maybe you'll still love to be here with me,
read this through,
sigh, sniff, sob on this page
and forget that you have to be strong.
Or maybe you'll call it a day,
put me and these words aside,
only to hurt a little less by it.
Maybe?
Maybe.

Nothing needed to be said,
though we spoke a word or two.
Silences also have their own language.
And at such nights they find their region.
You accepted it,
maybe out of guilt of not having anything to say
yourself
or the defeat that you were ready to swallow just so
that I could be the dominating one.
I would have walked into the nihility
but your eyes,
your eyes had a million things reserved.
But again,
nothing needed to be said.
You searched for your words in mine
and I was ready to offer even the last of my
recitations
and maybe if the night wasn't too cold
and my throat wasn't too dry,
I would have sung you a song.
This conversation between us,
it's no towel soaked dry with our tears that we let
hang on the hook,

or the flower you pick out of a bouquet to let wither
in your vase.
It has to be said,
it has to be ironed,
folded,
kept in the cupboard.
So tomorrow let's sit again,
let's say our salutations again,
let's allow this language to finally find its letters
and in that moment,
tell me again
how none of this can be expressed with mere words.
Tell me that love cannot be explained.

-to say or not to say

Dearest
Abbu

I have some of the fondest memories with him.
But they always coincide with a sense of a goodbye.
Like yesterday he was peeling an orange for me
and now when I look back at a plate full of love,
I see it rotting.
Yesterday he made me soup for my sore throat
and today I'm choking on my tears.
Yesterday he sat there
with one hand on his cheek reading my poems
and today nothing that I shout is reaching his ears.
Yesterday he held my hand so tight as if he'll never
let it go and today I'm forgetting his touch.
Yesterday,
just about time yesterday,
he held me in his arms for the first time and
welcomed me into this world
and today I have to let him go from here forever.

-goodbye, Abbu

My ammi jaan's name translates to "illumination".
For a light to give birth to the tiny flicker that I am,
my only hope is that I can light up the world one day
as bright as the al-Noor of her heart irradiates mine.

-Afroz

It’s true when they say that the pen is the mightiest
sword.
I don’t know how many stories I have sculpted
out of innocent people
and wrote them down in inks of contempt,
a rotting sanctuary,
and a sweet haunting bloodshed.
Sometimes romanticizing the voids of their soul,
other times leaving a mark on their already scarred
heart,
are poets really that callous.
And if yes,
how is it that we break our own hearts in the
process?
Are we healing our hearts by lauding your miseries,
while all we ever wished was to let you let go of the
pain?

- are we hurting you?

My mother used to take care of every formality of a
claimed or unclaimed dead body.
Clean them,
wash them,
pray for them
and wish her final goodbye.
She would make sure all the mourners ate
and no one cried loud enough for the spirit of the
dead to be hurt.
Unless,
she had to do it for the one man she ever loved.
The faces of half a dozen dead hovered over her head
but that day no one else mattered.
The wind hit the finality of a departure on a face that
had become numb.
The janaza couldn't be proceeded,
the weight of my mother's sorrow kept pulling the
body back to the ground,
as if to say just lay down here in my arms one last
time. Coaxing the tender but soulless body,
she held his feet,
as if to beg,
please let me die with you today

and not break our promise
of living in this world together if at all.
That day my mother didn’t care who ate,
that day she didn’t know which prayer would work,
until then my mother saw death,
but that day my mother felt death.

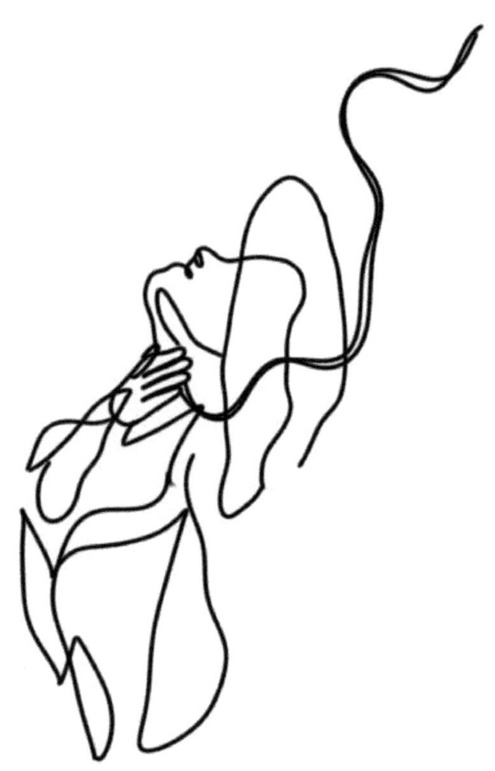

ENCOMIUM

I strangle my neck with my slender hands,
in hopes that it shall stop the poison
that is so intensely and dangerously awaiting
to escape my virulent throat

I do not speak of civility or morality,
of pleading or cleansing,
I speak of harsh truths
Of hunger unfed
Of seeds unwatered
Of love unrequited
Of choices condemned
Of a paradox called war at the cost of life.

Because everyone is told to speak of goodness.

A little of what makes you human:

your crooked smile/ your unceasing agony/ your venture through it/ the last slice of pizza you give up for someone/ the feeling of longing-ness that throbs within you/ your need to be accepted/ your self-sufficiency/ your day dreams/ the need to be someone else for yourself/ changing for them/ the way you pet dogs/ the check-in text you drop your distant friend/ staying awake to hear stories at 4am/ your apologies/not wanting enough/ wishing to once have the whole world/ you/ irony.

If the fierceness of a woman resuscitates,
these howling creatures will deteriorate to a hush.
The phoenix will burn a shade lighter,
for the power of a woman
lights up brighter than the fire in hell.

ENCOMIUM

I think it's a lie to believe that people in love,
love the other unconditionally
with all their imperfections
and things that they are insecure of.

Because I'm scared to stand on your left
knowing that the vulnerabilities of my heart
show clearly on the right side of my face
with a little mole that doesn't add anything but obscurity.

I'm scared to let you look too deep in my eyes
that aren't hazel, amber or scarlet colored
but a deep rustic brown that looks like blood that dried but could never heal.

I'm scared to smile or laugh too hard on jokes you make to lighten my heart,
knowing that it's unreserved,
and it makes my eyes shrink so small
that you won't be able to see if it's genuine.

ENCOMIUM

I'm scared to let you kiss my forehead
dreading that you'll know it's full of craters
that has been holding onto everything
that I should have let gone.

I'm scared to let you feel the warmth of my hand for
too long in the fear that every burning desire of mine
will bruise you a little.

And when you tell me that you want to hug me long
enough to never let go,
I'm scared that I'll melt into you and lose my
composure and you'll know that I was never so
strong.

And yet,
it's hard to not let myself be bare
and open
and free
and defenseless,
for if not even you,
who will love me otherwise?

Sorry

ENCOMIUM

I'm sorry
you couldn't see me become what you wanted me to be.
I'm sorry
you knew me but only as a daughter.
You didn't see me shed the insecurities,
or the scars that my skin bore for ages.
I'm not just smiles and poetry now, Dad.
I'm so much more, on a path that a 21 year old could create. I'm a lost childhood,
a yearning teenage,
and a troubled adulthood.
And yet I believe I'm made for bigger things
because you told me so.
I'm sorry
that you didn't see me learn how to live on my own
because that is what life demands of now.
Maybe if you would have, you would have been proud.
It's a shame how far we are,
and yet I've never felt closer to you than now.
How I couldn't hug you one last time,
or hold you in your most fragile times,
I'm sorry I felt so small,
I'm sorry I was so incapable.
You couldn't see me beg on nights alone

and silence the severity of a violent scream from my
mouth which came after everything was lost.
Had you been able to,
you would have known,
I learnt patience from you.
I'm sorry Dad,
I could be nothing more.
And I'm sorry,
there's only nothingness left.

ENCOMIUM

And tonight you're far away,
in the arms of someone strange,
on a bed of different flowers,
and you just grow farther, away.
And tomorrow the night shall see,
a love that's new and free,
from a heart that once belonged,
In a field of dying storm.
But just so you know,
in every misery and the low,
I shall be right here,
if you,
decide to come back from the blue.
Under a sky of howling stars,
the ones we named ours,
and a moon that sees me wail,
tonight I shall wait.

-a song that turned into poetry

Your power over me was a rare offering.
Or maybe a malediction, not that I could tell.
I was too consumed
under the oath of bringing your identity to life in mine
and to reason my rumination in terms with you.
But tell me,
would it be too astonishing to exclaim,
after my soulful concede to you,
I hadn't even ever met you.

ENCOMIUM

Overtime I've realized,
to be a poet there has to be a few requirements.
A craving in the heart. Not necessarily of love. But
anything at all.
A lost someone,
a lost someplace,
a lost self.
A gone friend,
a gone memory,
a gone ambition.
A decreased appetite,
a decreased conviction,
a decreased space.
A broken limb,
a broken bond,
a broken dream.
A seasonal depression,
a seasonal healing,
a seasonal damage.
Overtime I've realized,
to be a poet you have to have a lot of loss as a pre
requisite.
As if to be a poet is to be persistently,
obnoxiously
excruciatingly tormented.

I recite a silent prayer when I hear of someone's
death,
almost as if it strikes me personally.
Like I can hear the rush of their family's' footsteps to
enter the emergency rooms and the way it would
drag after every hope is lost.
Like I can close my eyes and touch their hands and
know that it's pale and lifeless and cold as if I had
held it forever and knew it to be warm.
I can hear loud and silent,
meaningful and empathizing wails of people
surrounding the dead.
I can see the body is heavy,
I can see the air is suffocating
and I can see that in another few minutes everything
will dissipate into nothingness.
I can see death closely,
I can see myself next to the dead
and I can see you in every death.

A concept:

You say you know a place that's five songs away from your home.
So I play another two and reach you.
We sit in your car and its seats are cold as if they've been waiting for us.
You allow me to play the radio and it's the song that you had shared with me for the very first time.
I smile a little without looking at you,
you turn towards the window looking at the reflection of me. We don't hold hands,
we don't speak much,
and I don't ask where we are headed.
I allow this space and time,
I allow you and this song
to have every part of me in this moment.
A moment that I know is going to last only for another four songs,
a moment in which I knew these songs are telling me that you love me.

-drive away

Where does hope come from:

shared umbrellas / offered metro seals / an advanced position in the queue/ a vehicle letting you pass / an ear that listens/ someone's reassurances/ answered miracles after tragedies/organ donors at hospitals/ the birth of a child while there is no guarantee of an existing world tomorrow.

One day,
you'll want to stop cutting yourself
with the sharp edges of a man who couldn't offer
humility and grace.
One day,
you'll not want a fire,
the woods,
the hunting
or the haunting.
Men whose eyes are oceans
but nothing like the sunset above it.
Men who avert from acknowledgment and
submersion into your voice,
men who place broken bottles on your chest as if
they are awarding you with the pain.
Men who are draped in flames of meaningless
warmth,
whose touch feels like a scar
whose embrace feels like iron bars
and whose hands have done everything but held you
when you needed it the most.
One day,
you'll want a love that feels safe,
a love that is as simple as this one sentence:
a love you deserve.

One day,
you'll want a love that is like the rain washing away
the fire.
A love that insists you love yourself more.
A love that is the silver lining,
a shadow that stays,
a love that's tender,
unravelling the knots of pain,
one that looks like it has swallowed light and life.
And one day you'll get this love.
Until then, wait.

Rest
in
Peace

The phrase toq- bor-neh translates to "you bury me",
which is to say,
this world would be like that devoid of its element
if I were to lose you.
My beloved, it'll hurt me to see you tormented
but your hands need to bury me.
Let me love you until my grave has been dug
and you've lowered me down.
Let your eyes be the last pair I see
before these pools are drought forever.
Let these fingers be the tasbeeh
which beckon Al- Bāsit to extend your life
before they are cold and unwavering.
Let my Ṣalāt al-Janāzah be orchestrated by you.
My beloved,
let me die before you.

ENCOMIUM

When an era would have been passed,
when libraries would have been demolished to make complexes,
when forests would have been cleared to construct warm residences,
and when books would have been bargained against for money,
when 2021 would be a century past,
I still would like to be remembered.
Which is why, I write.
On tree barks,
and shells across the beaches,
on cemented benches
and on window sills of my classroom,
on a flying leaf
and on the stones of graveyards.
Because when everything would have passed,
I hope these will stay
and what's a better identity for a poet
to be known if not for her poems.

As we draw nearer to an end,
I place every emotion
that of happiness
sorrow
hunger
into the two palms of your hand that hold me and my work with such tenderness
just like a child would be held by its mother.
As a poet, I give birth to poetry and as I hand it over to you,
I hope you'll let it grow with you,
nourish it,
and love it.

-khuda hafiz
(until we meet again)

ABOUT THE AUTHOR

Ermina Afroz is a 21 year old writer and modern day artist, currently pursuing triple majors in Psychology, Journalism and Literature. Her work revolves around various themes but mostly around loss, love and longing. She has elements of both personal experience depicted through her writings as well as poems that she writes as an ode to others, human or nature. A similar composition was narrated in her debut book, Comma, that she self-published in 2020. Encomium however, becomes more personal to her since it is dedicated to her father, who graciously fought the battles of covid and passed away in 2021.

OTHER BOOKS BY THE AUTHOR

SPECIAL THANKS TO THE ILLUSTRATOR: ZAINAB SHABIR

Thank you for bringing the poems to life by the beautifully curated illustrations, most of which are so realistic to the times for which it is drawn and has minute intricate details close to my heart. Thank you for the constant reassurances with the vague ideas in mind that you so effortlessly brought down on paper. This couldn't have been done better by anyone else.

-from Ermina

ENCOMIUM

9 798890 660312

Printed by Libri Plureos GmbH in Hamburg,
Germany